My New Book of Words 2

Nina Gontar

New South Wales

Name: _____

My New Book of Words 2: New South Wales

Text: Nina Gontar
Illustrations: Nina Gontar
Editor: Jarrah Moore
Designer: Karen Mayo
Production controller: Renee Cusmano

Acknowledgements
Dedicated to Vanessa, a true friend.

Text © 2012 Nina Gontar
Illustrations © 2012 Nina Gontar

ISBN 978 0 17 018859 3

Cengage Learning Australia
Level 7, 80 Dorcas Street
South Melbourne, Victoria Australia 3205
Phone: 1300 790 853

Cengage Learning New Zealand
Unit 4B Rosedale Office Park
331 Rosedale Road, Albany, North Shore NZ 0632
Phone: 0800 449 725

For learning solutions, visit **cengage.com.au**

Printed in China by RR Donnelley Asia Printing Solutions Limited
1 2 3 4 5 6 7 16 15 14 13 12

Contents

Building Sounds

ang sang	**ing** thing	**ong** song	**ung** flung

ack black	**eck** neck	**ick** stick	**ock** clock	**uck** duck

all ball	**ell** fellow	**ill** silly	**oll** follow	**ull** pull

sh shut	**th** thank	**ch** chicken	**wh** when	**tch** ditch

A	**ai** train	**ay** stay	**a_e** cake	**a** angel

E	**ee** feeds	**ea** teacher	**e_e** theme	**e** she

I	**igh** night	**y** fly	**i_e** inside	**i** Friday

O	**oa** boat	**ow** show	**o_e** home	**o** go

U	**ew** new	**oo** boot	**u_e** flute	**u** music

Add **s** stars	Add **es** bushes	Add **ed** talked	Add **ly** quickly	Add **est** loudest	Add **ing** talking

ou house

ow brown

ar barked

a mask

eer deer

ear hear

oy boy

oi coin

ea head

ie friendly

a many

air hairy

ear wear

are share

ere there

ir first

er her

ur turn

or world

ore more

aw crawl

our four

oor door

oar roar

Annoying amphibians make alligators angry.

a	b	c
above		Adelaide
across		Antarctica
aeroplane		Anzac Day
after		Arctic Ocean
afternoon		
again		
almost		
also		
animal		
another		
answer		
anything		
around		
asked		
asleep		
ate		
away		

Bashful brown bears like to hide behind balloons.

beautiful

because

began

behind

believe

beneath

beside

between

bicycle

blind

born

bought

boyfriend

breakfast

brought

build

buy

Bathurst

Bondi Beach

Brisbane

Broken Hill

Clowns climb with care onto colourful cans.

called		celery	Canada
came		cents	Capricorn
carried		circle	Celsius
castle		circus	Chinese New Year
caught		city	
clean			
close			
clothes			
coming			
computer			
contact			
corner			
could			
cousin			
crawl			
cried			
cry			

d D

Don't disturb dogs when they're dancing to hip-hop.

dangerous

date

dear

decided

dictionary

different

digital

dirty

disappear

dodge

does

done

drain

dream

drink

drive

drought

Denmark

DNA

Dreamtime

Dubbo

Energetic elephants enjoy exercising.

each		Earth
early		East Timor
eat		Egypt
edge		Ethiopia
either		
email		
enormous		
enough		
environment		
even		
every		
everybody		
everyone		
everything		
everywhere		
exciting		
explain		

A fairy's favourite food is fairy floss.

faced			February
family			Fiji
farmed			France
fast			Fremantle
favourite			
few			
finally			
find			
finish			
first			
for			
found			
friend			
frighten			
front			
full			
funny			

Gigantic gorillas like to graze on green grass.

game			Galaxy
garage			Great Barrier Reef
gave			Greece
getting			Guatemala
girlfriend			
given			
glasses			
glitter			
glue			
goes			
gone			
good			
goodbye			
great			
group			
grow			
guess			

h H

Horses in hats hold their heads up high.

hair
happened
happily
happy
hard
have
having
head
heard
heavy
height
here
hero
holiday
how
hungry
hurtful

Haiti
Halloween
Hawaii
Hong Kong

Interesting insects are everywhere!

ice	
ignore	
imagination	
imagine	
important	

include		
incorrect		
insect		
inside		
instant		
instead		
interesting		
invisible		
invitation		
issue		
itchy		
itself		

ice-cream
idea
idol
iron
island

I'd
India
Internet
Italy

j **J**

Joeys in jackets just jump and jump and jump.

jacket

jaw

jealous

jeans

jeer

jellyfish

jewellery

join

joke

journal

journey

judge

juice

juicy

jumped

jungle

just

Jakarta

Jamaica

Japan

Jupiter

k   **K**

Do kind kangaroos like to kiss cute koalas?

keen		knew	Katoomba
keenly		knit	Kenya
keep		knock	Korea
kept		know	Kuwait
key		knowledge	
kicking			
kill			
kilt			
kind			
kindergarten			
kindness			
kingdom			
kissed			
kit			
kitchen			
kite			
kitten			

l L

Large lions laugh at little lions licking lollipops.

lady

large

last

lately

laugh

learnt

leave

letter

light

likely

listen

lived

loose

lose

loud

love

lucky

Launceston

Leo

Libra

Libya

Mischievous mermaids cause magical mix-ups.

machine
made
magic
make
making
many
measure
message
might
mistake
money
more
morning
most
mother
much
myself

Miss
Mr
Mrs
Ms

n   N

Never number noodles!

name
narrow
near
need
nest
never
new
next
nice
night
no
nobody
none
nose
nothing
now
nowhere

New Zealand
North Pole
November
Nullarbor Plain

Oscar the octopus only eats oranges.

oblong
ocean
offer
often
once
only
open
opposite
or
other
otherwise
our
ourselves
outside
over
owe
own

Oceania
October
Olympics
Orion

p | P

Parrots, pigs and pelicans make perfect pets for pirates.

parents
party
past
pencil
people
picture
piece
place
playground
please
pool
present
printer
probably
pull
push
put

Paris
Peru
Pisces
Pluto

The quiet queen quite enjoys a quick game of quoits.

qualify

quality

quantity

quarrel

quarter

queen

question

queue

quick

quickest

quiet

quietly

quilt

quit

quite

quiz

quote

Quebec

Queensland

Queenstown

Rollerblading rabbits race faster than robots.

rabbit

rare

rather

ready

really

receive

rectangle

remember

rescue

return

rhyme

right

roll

room

rough

round

rush

Romania

Rugby League

Rugby Union

Russia

Slithering snakes hiss when sausages sizzle.

said		Saturn
sandwich		South Australia
save		South Pole
saw		Sydney
scary		
school		
sentence		
should		
show		
sister		
skid		
slide		
someone		
something		
sometimes		
stayed		
suddenly		

Tiny tortoises are trying to trap a tarantula.

take
taste
telephone
television
thank
their
there
these
they
thought
through
together
told
tomorrow
tonight
tried
turn

Tasman Sea
Taurus
Tokyo
Townsville

25

U

Umbrellas go up, and we go under!

ugly	
umpire	
unable	
uncomfortable	
underneath	
understand	
undo	
uniform	
unit	
unless	
until	
upon	
upset	
upstairs	
use	
useful	
usual	

Uganda
Ukraine
Uranus
Uruguay

Vegetables in vases look very peculiar.

vacation

valley

valuable

various

verb

vegetable

vehicle

vertical

veterinarian

video

view

violin

visit

visitor

voice

volcano

vote

Venus

Victoria

Viking

Virgo

Why would a walrus wash a whale with a washcloth?

walk			Wagga Wagga
want			Wales
warm			Wednesday
was			Wellington
watch			
water			
wear			
weather			
weekend			
were			
without			
woke			
woman			
won			
wonderful			
work			
would			

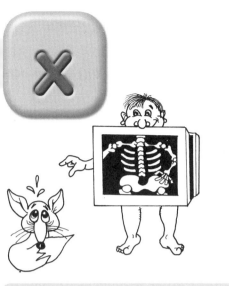

axed   X-ray

exit   xylophone

fixing

pixel

pixie

sixth

sixty

X-ray the fox next, please.

yacht

yard

year

yesterday

yoghurt

you

your

Your yoyo broke
the yellow vase.

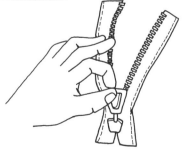

zebra

zero

zigzag

zone

zoo

zoom

zucchini

Zip up the zipper!

Abbreviations

N	north	ASAP	as soon as possible	BCE	before Common Era
S	south	DOB	date of birth	CE	Common Era
E	east	ETA	estimated time of arrival		
W	west	PTO	Please turn over.	Dr	Doctor
		RSVP	Please reply.	jr	junior
				MP	Member of Parliament
Ave	Avenue			PM	Prime Minister
Blvd	Boulevard	etc.	and so on	Prof.	Professor
Dr.	Drive	e.g.	for example	rep.	representative
St	Street	i.e.	that is	sr	senior
Rd	Road	no.	number		

Actions

abuse	dance	ignite	paddle	tackle
accept	destroy	ignore	poke	talk
admire	drive	imagine	pretend	tidy
bathe	fetch	laugh	raid	uncover
bite	fight	leap	rejoice	undo
build	follow	lunge	relax	unfold
capture	gallop	march	scare	watch
climb	grasp	mend	search	whisper
cuddle	grumble	move	shake	wreck

Add an Ending

word	-er	-est	-ly
dense	denser	densest	densely
fierce	fiercer	fiercest	fiercely
funny	funnier	funniest	funnily
happy	happier	happiest	happily
loud	louder	loudest	loudly
merry	merrier	merriest	merrily
pretty	prettier	prettiest	prettily
smooth	smoother	smoothest	smoothly
warm	warmer	warmest	warmly

Can you think of some more?

 **Sounds**

ai

bait	grain
claim	hail
fail	tail
frail	wait

snails

ay

always	play
clay	relay
hay	stay
Monday	yesterday

birthday

a_e

ate	plate
cake	same
crane	shame
late	tame

snakes

a

able	lady
baby	radio
capable	staples
fable	table

labels

Better Words

big	little	nice	said	went
colossal	insignificant	courteous	answered	crawled
enlarged	miniature	delicious	asked	dawdled
enormous	minor	delightful	called	jogged
giant	petite	enjoyable	explained	moved
gigantic	short	friendly	mentioned	proceeded
huge	slight	kind	mumbled	raced
immense	small	pleasant	murmured	ran
large	teeny	polite	replied	tiptoed
massive	tiny	tasty	shouted	walked
vast	young	wonderful	whispered	wandered

Birds

bellbird	eagle	lorikeet	quail	swallow
bowerbird	emu	lyrebird	robin	thrush
brolga	finch	magpie	sparrow	wagtail
canary	galah	nightingale	stork	wren
cockatoo	heron	owl		
crane	jay	parrot		
crow	kingfisher	peacock		
dove	kiwi	pelican		
duck	kookaburra	pigeon		

ch Sounds

ch

beaches   crunch
chain   march
chalk   peach
champion   reaches
cheat   speech
choose   teacher

cheese

tch

batch   matchstick
catcher   patch
crutches   pitcher
ditch   stitch
hatching   stretch
match   watch

witch

t

actually   fracture
adventure   future
capture   mixture
century   nature
creature   picture
eventually   temperature

statue

Compound Words

after + noon = _____

any + one = _____

birth + day = _____

candle + light = _____

grand + child = _____

grand + father = _____

grand + mother = _____

home + work = _____

human + kind = _____

jelly + fish = _____

lip + stick = _____

neck + lace = _____

out + side = _____

play + ground = _____

pop + corn = _____

rain + coat = _____

sand + castle = _____

some + body = _____

some + one = _____

tooth + brush = _____

water + fall = _____

candlelight

Computers

address	desktop	install	scanner
back up	disk	Internet	scroll
bit	disk drive	keyboard	search
blog	document	laptop	server
broadband	dot com	megabyte	shortcut
byte	download	memory stick	software
cancel	file	menu bar	space bar
CD-ROM	firewall	modem	tab
cell	gigabyte	mousepad	typing
chatting	hard drive	network	USB port
Command key	hardware	printer	virus
connection	home page	program	website
cursor	icon	RAM	
database	ink cartridge	ROM	

Email

account	directory	mail	settings
attachment	draft	message	signature
calendar	events	open	spam
contact list	folders	password	storage
communication	junk	receive	webmail
delete	log in	send	write

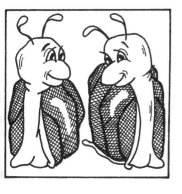

Contractions

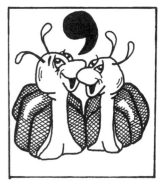

Join two words to make a contraction, and don't forget the **apostrophe**.

could have	could've	they are	they're
could not	couldn't	they had	they'd
does not	doesn't	they have	they've
do not	don't	they will	they'll
had not	hadn't	we are	we're
he has	he's	we had	we'd
he is	he's	we have	we've
he will	he'll	we will	we'll
he would	he'd	we would	we'd
I am	I'm	were not	weren't
I have	I've	what is	what's
I will	I'll	where is	where's
I would	I'd	who has	who's
must not	mustn't	who is	who's
she has	she's	who would	who'd
she is	she's	will not	won't
she will	she'll	would not	wouldn't
she would	she'd	you have	you've
there is	there's	you will	you'll
there will	there'll	you would	you'd

 # Sounds

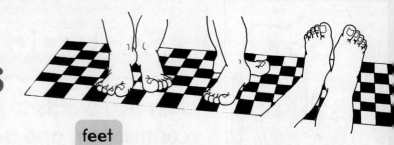

feet

ee

betw*ee*n	k*ee*ping
d*ee*pest	m*ee*ting
f*ee*ling	s*ee*n
gr*ee*nest	wh*ee*l

seals

ea

b*ea*ch	r*ea*ding
*ea*ch	r*ea*son
n*ea*tly	s*ea*side
pl*ea*se	t*ea*ching

recycle

e

b*e*	r*e*cent
b*e*ing	r*e*mix
d*e*tour	sh*e*
h*e*	w*e*

e_e

athl*e*t*e*	sc*e*n*e*
concr*e*t*e*	supr*e*m*e*
del*e*t*e*	th*e*m*e*
extr*e*m*e*	th*e*s*e*

compete

Exercise

aerobics

archery

athletics

ballet

ballroom dancing

baseball

basketball

BMX racing

canoeing

car racing

cricket

cycling

fishing

football

gymnastics

hang-gliding

hockey

horseriding

jogging

judo

karate

kayaking

mountaineering

netball

parachuting

polo

rockclimbing

rollerblading

rowing

sailing

skating

skiing

snowboarding

soccer

softball

squash

surfing

swimming

tenpin bowling

volleyball

walking

water polo

weightlifting

wrestling

 **Sounds**

ph

al**ph**abet	**ph**rase
gra**ph**	**ph**ysical
pam**ph**let	saxo**ph**one
phone	s**ph**ere
photocopy	trium**ph**
photograph	tro**ph**y

dol**ph**in

_____

_____

_____

_____

gh

cou**gh**	rou**gh**
cou**gh**ed	rou**gh**er
cou**gh**ing	rou**gh**ly
enou**gh**	tou**gh**
lau**gh**ing	tou**gh**er
lau**gh**ter	tou**gh**est

lau**gh**

_____

_____

_____

_____

ff

bu**ff**alo	flu**ff**y
cu**ff**	gra**ff**iti
di**ff**erent	pu**ff**y
di**ff**icult	scru**ff**y
e**ff**ect	to**ff**ee
flu**ff**	tra**ff**ic

sni**ff**ing

_____

_____

_____

_____

Family	Friends	Favourite Food

Fantasy

Once upon a time ...

adventure

alien

battle

defend

dream

enchantress

fairytale

galaxy

giant

goblin

hero

heroine

imagination

legend

magic

magical

make believe

mermaid

monster

myth

prince

princess

protect

robot

space

superhero

unicorn

vampire

villain

wizard

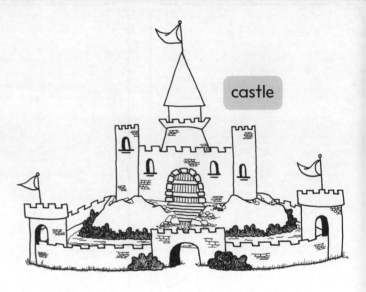
castle

dragon

... happily ever after.

leprechaun

knight

Feelings

Angry

annoyed
bitter
cross
enraged
fiery
furious
mad

Happy

cheerful
delighted
glad
jolly
joyful
overjoyed
thrilled

Sad

distressed
downcast
gloomy
glum
sorrowful
troubled
upset

Concerned

alarmed
anxious
bothered
nervous
troubled
uneasy
worried

Impatient

eager
excited
hasty
hurried
impetuous
irritated
keen

Scared

afraid
fearful
frightened
panicky
petrified
startled
terrified

Embarrassed

ashamed
awkward
humiliated
mortified
self-conscious
tongue-tied
uncomfortable

Proud

complacent
conceited
content
pleased
satisfied
smug
vain

Surprised

amazed
astonished
astounded
flabbergasted
shocked
startled
stunned

Fractions

A fraction is what you get when you divide something into smaller equal parts.

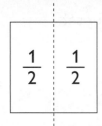

$\frac{1}{2}$ = one-half

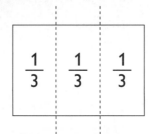

$\frac{1}{3}$ = one-third

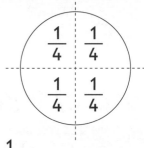

$\frac{1}{4}$ = one-quarter

A fraction is written as two numbers, one above and one below the line.

$\frac{1}{4}$

⟵ This number is the **numerator**.

⟵ This number is the **denominator**.

The numerator tells you how many parts there are.
The denominator tells you how many parts you would need to make a whole.

$\frac{1}{4}$ = one-quarter

$\frac{2}{4}$ = two-quarters

$\frac{3}{4}$ = three-quarters

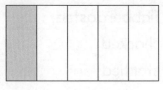

$\frac{1}{5}$ = one-fifth

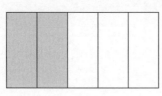

$\frac{2}{5}$ = two-fifths

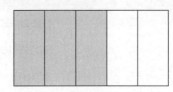

$\frac{3}{5}$ = three-fifths

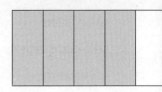

$\frac{4}{5}$ = four-fifths

Government

- [ ] Australian Greens
- [ ] Australian Labor Party
- [ ] Liberal Party of Australia
- [ ] National Party of Australia

community
Constitution
councillor
democracy
deputy lord mayor
election
governor-general
independent
lord mayor
mayor
minister

Opposition
Parliament
party
politician
premier
prime minister
Senate
senator
shire council
treasurer
vote

Assembly
Cabinet
chairperson
committee

Grammar

adjective
adverb
clause
collective noun
conjunction
connective
future tense
homophone

noun
paragraph
past tense
phrase
plural
preposition
present tense
pronoun

proper noun
question
sentence
singular
statement
tense
title
verb

Homophones

ate	I **ate** my dinner.
eight	She has **eight** dogs.

be	It will **be** sunny today.
bee	A **bee** can sting you.

berry	I will eat the **berry**.
bury	Dogs **bury** bones.

blew	I **blew** lots of bubbles.
blue	Is the sky **blue**?

brake	My bike has a **brake**.
break	Did you **break** the cup?

buy	Go and **buy** an apple.
by	I run **by** myself.

chews	The cow **chews** grass.
choose	**Choose** me, please.

dear	**Dear** Santa …
deer	A **deer** has hooves.

die	Plants **die** without water.
dye	I will **dye** my pants red.

eye	My **eye** is sore.
I	**I** am a happy person.

flour	I use **flour** to make cakes.
flower	The **flower** smells lovely.

for	I will go **for** a walk.
four	Two plus two equals **four**.

hair	My **hair** is curly.
hare	The **hare** can run quickly.

hear	I can **hear** the song playing.
here	Come **here**, please.

knew	I **knew** his name.
new	That toy is **new**.

knight	The **knight** sits on a horse.
night	At **night** I sleep in my bed.

know	I **know** my age.
no	Yes is the opposite of **no**.

knows	She **knows** her address.
nose	My **nose** is itchy!

made	I **made** my own bed.
maid	The **maid** washed the dishes.

mail	I will **mail** the letter.
male	A **male** duck is a drake.

meat	Do you eat red **meat**?
meet	**Meet** me at the zoo.

oar	In my boat is an **oar**.
or	Do you prefer red **or** blue?

one	I have **one** nose.
won	Who **won** the race?

pair	I own a **pair** of sneakers.
pear	I ate a **pear** at lunchtime.

plain	I like **plain** sandwiches.
plane	The **plane** flew away.

read	I have **read** this book.
red	My apple is **red**.

right	Will you go left or **right**?
write	I love to **write** stories.

road	The **road** was bumpy.
rode	I **rode** my horse today.

sail	My boat has a white **sail**.
sale	My computer was on **sale**.

scent	This rose has a **scent**.
sent	Mum **sent** me shopping.

sea	Fish swim in the **sea**.
see	I can **see** the mountains.

sew	I **sew** with a needle.
so	I am **so** hungry.

some	Would you like **some** fruit?
sum	One plus one is a **sum**.

son	Her **son** is a clever boy.
sun	The **sun** is up in the sky.

tail	My dog's **tail** is so long.
tale	A **tale** is a story.

their	That is **their** car.
there	Go over **there**!

waist	My belt goes around my **waist**.
waste	Don't **waste** water!

wear	I **wear** a school uniform.
where	**Where** is my dog?

which	**Which** hat do you like?
witch	A **witch** can do magic.

wood	I put **wood** on the fire.
would	**Would** you like to play?

Sounds

i

bicycle   kindest

blind   mind

child   triangle

find   wild

spiders

i_e

fine   quite

grime   shine

inside   time

pile   write

smiles

igh

bright   might

fight   nightmare

high   right

lightning   tight

night

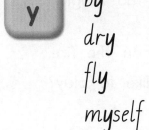

y

by   shy

dry   sky

fly   try

myself   why

cry

"ie" or "ei"?

Put "i" before "e" ...

achieve	brief	niece	thief
belief	chief	piece	thieves
believe	grief	relief	unbelievable

... except after "c" ...

ceiling	conceive	deceive	receipt
conceit	deceit	inconceivable	receive
conceited	deceitful	perceive	receiving

... when the sound you hear is "ee".
But not when it's "ay", as in "neighbour" or "weigh".

eight	freight	sleigh	vein
eighty	reins	veil	weight

While these words tease and just do as they please!

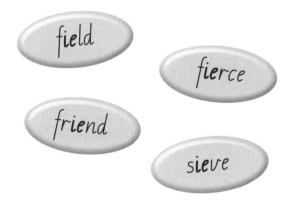

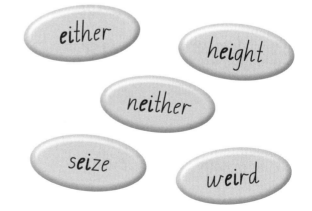

49

 **Sounds**

giraffes

 g

engine	germ
gem	giant
general	gigantic
generally	ginger
generous	magic
gentle	magician

oranges

ge

age	language
arrange	large
bandage	page
change	stage
charge	strange
garbage	village

bridge

dge

badge	hedge
dodge	judge
edge	ledge
fidget	porridge
fridge	ridge
gadget	wedge

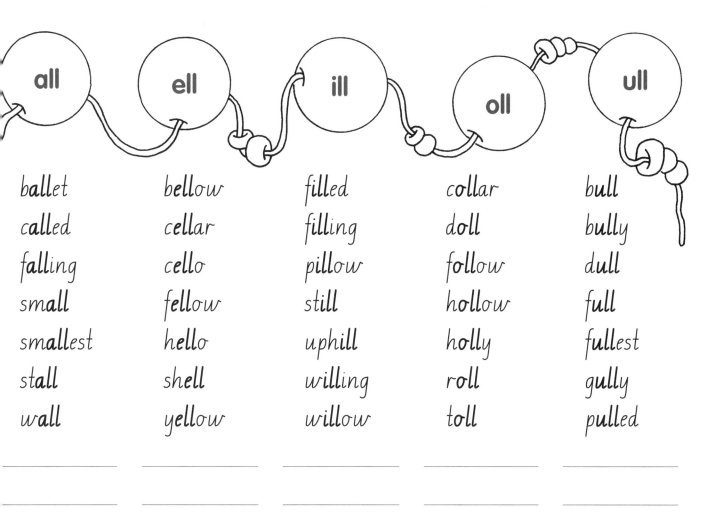

all	ell	ill	oll	ull
ballet	bellow	filled	collar	bull
called	cellar	filling	doll	bully
falling	cello	pillow	follow	dull
small	fellow	still	hollow	full
smallest	hello	uphill	holly	fullest
stall	shell	willing	roll	gully
wall	yellow	willow	toll	pulled

Liquids

apple cider	cream	lemonade	sauce
bleach	custard	milk	shampoo
blood	detergent	milkshake	soft drink
brake fluid	fruit juice	mineral water	soup
broth	fruit punch	nail polish	soy sauce
bubble bath	ginger beer	oil	tea
coffee	green tea	paint	tears
conditioner	handwash	perfume	vinegar
cordial	honey	petrol	water

Maths

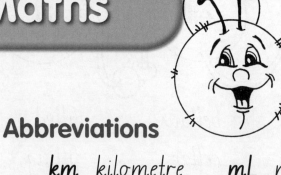

10 ten
20 twenty
30 thirty
40 forty
50 fifty
60 sixty
70 seventy
80 eighty
90 ninety
100 one hundred
1000 one thousand
1000 000 one million

Abbreviations

C	Celsius	km	kilometre	mL	millilitre
cm	centimetre	L	litre	mm	millimetre
g	gram	m	metre	sec.	second
hr	hour	mg	milligram	vol.	volume
kg	kilogram	min.	minute		

Vocabulary

add	fraction	radius
amount	graph	scales
angle	height	solid
area	horizontal	square
calculator	length	subtract
cents	line	temperature
circumference	measure	thermometer
cube	multiply	time
decimal	number	vertical
diameter	ordinal	volume
divide	pair	weigh
dollars	parallel	weight
equal	percentage	whole
estimate	perimeter	width

oa Sounds

o

go no
going ochre
gross only
most so

post

oa

boast goal
coat goat
float roast
foal toast

boat

o_e

alone note
cone phone
home stone
hope vote

rope

ow

crow low
flow mow
grow row
know show

bows

Other Sounds

Put the **b**ook down.

U	
bull	fullest
bullied	pull
bush	pulled
full	push

oo	
cook	looked
footpath	shook
good	stood
hood	took

The **c**ow is **ou**tside.

ow	
clown	now
down	power
growled	towel
how	wow

ou	
about	loudly
cloud	our
counting	round
found	sound

The **t**oy robot is **n**oisy.

oy	
annoy	joy
boy	joyful
destroy	oyster
enjoy	royal

oi	
avoid	point
choice	poison
disappoint	toilet
noise	voice

This is the **last jar**.

 a

ask	h**a**lf
br**a**ss	m**a**sk
f**a**st	p**a**ss
gr**a**ssy	p**a**st

 ar

b**ar**ked	c**ar**ve
b**ar**n	d**ar**ling
c**ar**pet	sn**ar**l
c**ar**toon	st**ar**ve

A **deer** app**ear**ed.

 eer

ch**eer**	sh**eer**
ch**eer**ful	st**eer**
j**eer**	v**eer**
p**eer**	volunt**eer**

ear

b**ear**d	g**ear**s
cl**ear**	h**ear**
d**ear**	n**ear**ly
f**ear**ed	y**ear**

Careful!
There's a **hairy bear**!

are

b**are**
b**are**ly
c**are**
d**are**
gl**are**
h**are**

ere

anywh**ere**
everywh**ere**
nowh**ere**
th**ere**
th**ere**fore
wh**ere**

air

ch**air**
d**air**y
f**air**
f**air**y
p**air**
st**air**s

ear

b**ear**
p**ear**
sw**ear**
t**ear**
t**ear**ing
w**ear**

Places to Visit

aquarium	Australian War Memorial	Lord Howe Island
art gallery	Blue Mountains	Luna Park
beach	Centennial Park	Murray River
botanical garden	Coober Pedy	Nullarbor Plain
lighthouse	Darling Harbour	Sydney Harbour Bridge
museum	Gold Coast	Tasmanian Wilderness
outback	Great Barrier Reef	Taronga Zoo
rainforest	Kakadu National Park	Three Sisters
theatre	Kimberley	Twelve Apostles
theme park	Lake Eyre	Uluru

People to Meet

architect	blueprints, bricks, buildings, cement, designs, drawings, plans
artist	brushes, canvas, chalk, charcoal, crayons, easel, paint, palette
baker	apron, baking, biscuits, bread, cakes, dough, flour, oven
chef	bake, boil, bowls, fry, kitchen, pans, recipe, refrigerator, stove
electrician	equipment, extension cord, pliers, tape, toolbox, van, wires
florist	arrangements, bouquets, flowers, fragrance, plants, ribbons
mechanic	engine, grease, oil, overalls, screwdriver, spanner, spark plug
plumber	blocked, dig, drain, excavate, pipes, sink, spade, toilet, water
police officer	accident, bikes, cars, law, offender, protect, station, thief, traffic
reporter	articles, interviews, investigation, magazine, newspaper, stories
writer	books, imagination, manuscript, paper, publish, story, typing

Punctuation Marks

, apostrophe

( ) brackets

Brackets go around extra information (like this bit).

● bullet point

: colon

, comma

A comma is a pause in a sentence, like this.

— dash

! exclamation mark

Use an exclamation mark when a sentence is exciting!

. full stop

Put a full stop at the end of a sentence.

? question mark

Where do you put a question mark?

" " quotation marks

/ slash

Repeat the Letter

bb — abbreviation, babble, bubble, bubblegum, cabbage, chubby, grubby, hobby, nibble, pebble, rabbit, ribbon, rubbish

cc — accelerate, accent, accept, acceptable, accessories, accident, accommodate, accompany, broccoli, hiccup, occur, success

dd — add, address, cuddle, giddy, hidden, ladder, middle, odd, paddle, paddock, peddle, puddle, riddle, suddenly

ff — affect, cliff, coffin, different, difficult, effect, fluffy, muffin, off, offend, offer, office, puff, puffy, ruffian, sniff, stuff, whiff

gg — biggest, dagger, digging, eggs, giggle, goggles, jogger, juggle, luggage, smuggle, snuggle, stagger, trigger, wiggle, wriggle

mm — clammy, comma, commercial, common, community, dummy, hammer, mammal, simmer, summer, tummy, yummy

nn — announce, annoy, antenna, banner, beginning, channel, dinner, goanna, granny, manners, nanny, spanner, tennis, winner

pp — appear, appearance, apple, apply, approach, approve, disappear, flippers, happen, happiness, happy, pepper, puppet

ss — across, address, bassinet, blossom, boss, chess, class, compass, dessert, fuss, glass, hiss, lesson, miss, mission, pass, toss

tt — attempt, better, bitter, clutter, glitter, kettle, kitty, letter, litter, little, mittens, mutter, pattern, rattle, settle, shatter, wattle

Schwa

Uh?

The letters **a, e, i, o, u** are called vowels, and they have lots of different sounds. Schwa is the lazy and quiet vowel sound you can hear in many words. Say the words "ago" and "dinner". Can you hear the "uh"? That's the schwa. Schwa sounds like "uh", no matter what vowel it is.

When you write a word with schwa in it, it's easy to get the spelling wrong, because all you can hear is the "uh" sound.

a	e	i	o	u
about	enough	decimal	actor	album
around	monster	easily	complete	bonus
balloon	sister	pencil	gallop	circus
banana	taken	terrible	harmony	picture
umbrella	winner	victim	mosquito	Uluru

Can you think of more words with the schwa sound?

sh Sounds

sh
fashion	pushing
friendship	rushed
gushing	shadow
mashed	shutting

fisherman

c
ancient	malicious
delicious	precious
efficient	suspicious
ferocious	vicious

liquorice

ss
assure	permission
discussion	possession
expression	pressure
mission	reassure

tissue

t
action	fraction
correction	multiplication
demolition	relaxation
education	subtraction

addition

Shapes and Objects

2D Shapes

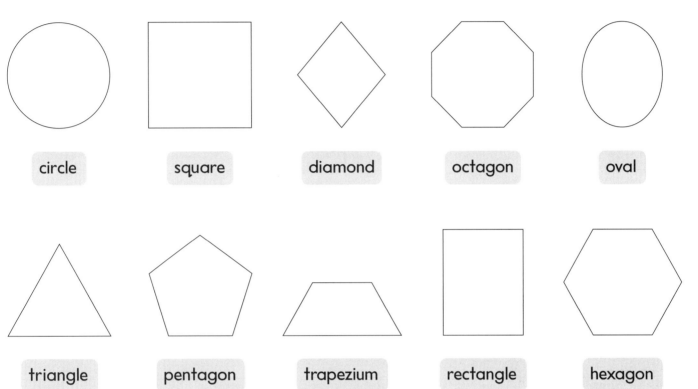

circle

square

diamond

octagon

oval

triangle

pentagon

trapezium

rectangle

hexagon

3D Objects

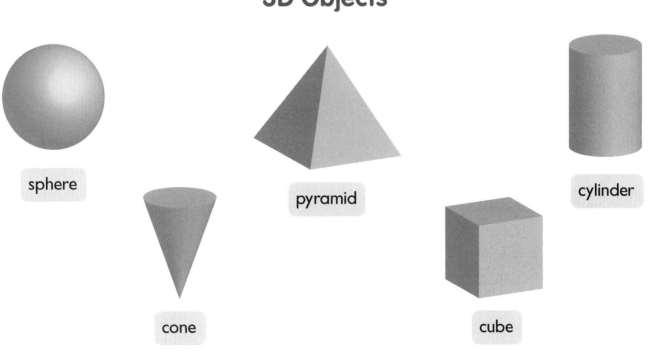

sphere

cone

pyramid

cube

cylinder

Silent Sounds

b
- bom**b**
- clim**b**
- com**b**
- crum**b**
- de**b**t
- dou**b**t
- dum**b**
- num**b**
- plum**b**er
- thum**b**

g
- desi**g**n
- **g**nash
- **g**naw
- **g**nome
- rei**g**n
- resi**g**n
- si**g**n

h
- **g**host
- **h**eir
- **h**onour
- **h**our
- w**h**at
- w**h**en
- w**h**ere
- w**h**ether
- w**h**ile
- w**h**ite
- w**h**y

gh
- bri**gh**t
- dau**gh**ter
- hei**gh**t
- hi**gh**
- nei**gh**bour
- ni**gh**t
- si**gh**
- si**gh**t
- sli**gh**t
- strai**gh**t
- tau**gh**t
- thou**gh**t
- wei**gh**

p
- cor**p**s
- cu**p**board
- **p**neumonia
- **p**sychiatrist
- **p**terodactyl
- ras**p**berry
- recei**p**t

t
- balle**t**
- buffe**t**
- cas**t**le
- croche**t**
- debu**t**
- depo**t**
- fas**t**en
- gourme**t**
- this**t**le
- vale**t**
- whis**t**le
- wres**t**ler

w
- ans**w**er
- s**w**ord
- t**w**o
- **w**ho
- **w**hole
- **w**hose
- **w**rap
- **w**reck
- **w**ren
- **w**restle
- **w**rist
- **w**ritten
- **w**rong
- **w**rote

k
- **k**nead
- **k**nee
- **k**new
- **k**nife
- **k**night
- **k**nit
- **k**nitting
- **k**nock
- **k**nuckle

Sounds

ss

across   dress
bossy   floss
class   lesson
crossed   pressed

address

_____
_____
_____

se

case   mouse
else   nurse
geese   purse
house   sense

horse

_____
_____
_____

ce

bounce   peace
dance   piece
glance   price
once   since

fence

_____
_____
_____

c

accent   circus
cents   citizen
cinema   city
circle   civilisation

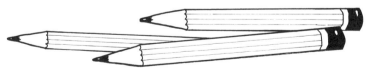

pencils

_____
_____
_____

Technology

Digital Camera

battery	focus	photo	shutter speed
buttons	format	pixel	storage
colours	image	printing	thumbnail
contrast	megapixel	red-eye	transfer
delete	memory card	resolution	upload
flash	mode	sensor	zoom

Video Game

adventure	joystick
audio	level
console	monitor
controller	multiplayer
gamepad	platform
handheld	player
interactive	television

MP3 Player

album	playlist
artist	previous track
audio file	rip
click wheel	scrolling
headphones	shuffle
next track	song
pause	volume

Mobile Phone

accessories	GPS navigation
address book	memo
calculator	ringtone
contact list	smartphone
conversation	text message

E-Reader

battery life	read
bookmark	reader
e-book	screen
format	stylus
novel	text size